My book of SOUNDS for READING

Letters and Their Combinations That
Make Two or More Sounds

NAOMI NAJERA PARDO

ISBN: Softcover   978-1-5144-8581-1
        EBook   978-1-5144-8580-4

Print information available on the last page

Rev. date: 04/20/2016

To order additional copies of this book, contact:
Xlibris
1-888-795-4274
www.Xlibris.com
Orders@Xlibris.com

My book of
SOUNDS for READING

INSTRUCTION MANUAL

Letters and Their Combinations That Make Two or More Sounds

Dedication

This book is dedicated to my wonderful husband Robin and my sons Isaac and Josiah, who have stood by me throughout the ups and downs of my life and have encouraged me in many ways in all my endeavors.(Philippians 4:13).

Acknowledgments

I would like to thank my 7th grade English teacher Sue Muller and my Liberal Studies professor Dr. Scott Waltz for proofreading my project and encouraging me to follow through with publishing it. Your help was invaluable to me!

Table of Contents

General Instructions

The lessons in this book are arranged so that the instructor will say the name of the letter(s) in the circle. Then present the lesson as it is written. Two or three lessons may be taught at a time. However, review is very essential.

Each day that new lessons are to be presented, one must review by beginning at the first lesson. You can say " This is the letter <u>A</u> (say the name), what are the sounds?" The students are then prompted to read the sounds in the boxes. Then you go on to lesson two and repeat the same procedure and so on until you get to the new lesson that's to be presented. It is necessary to repeat this process again after the new lessons are taught for reinforcement.

It is not necessary for kindergarteners or first graders to write the words that are above the boxes. However, they should be able to draw the letters in the boxes and color them. Second graders and up should be able to write the words above the boxes and underline the letter(s).

I have used the methods in this book with kindergarteners and all the way up to eighth graders. For the older students it is used as a method of intervention for those struggling in literacy. I have seen good improvement in their reading levels.

Supplies needed:

- 1 Instruction manual

- 1 workbook per student

- lead pencils

- coloring pencils or crayons in orange, yellow, light green, light blue and red which can be used to underline the letters in the words above the boxes.

LESSON 1 - LETTER <u>a</u>

The letter in the circle makes three different sounds: " a" as in apple, " a" as in April and "a" as in wanted. Instruct the students to draw a lowercase <u>a</u> in the first box and tell them that this letter makes the sound "a" as the sound of the first letter in the word apple. Color the box light green to represent the short vowel sound. Say the sound "a" as in <u>apple</u>.

In the second box draw an uppercase <u>A</u> and a lowercase <u>a</u>. This makes the sound "a" as the sound of the first letter in the word April. Color the box yellow to represent the long vowel sound. Say the sound "a" as in <u>April</u>.

In the third box draw a lowercase <u>a</u>. This letter makes the sound "a" as the sound of the <u>a</u> in the word wanted. Color the box orange. Say the sound "a" as in <u>wanted</u>.

Repeat the three sounds of the letter <u>a</u>.

For older students have them write the words above each box and underline the letter <u>a</u> in each word.

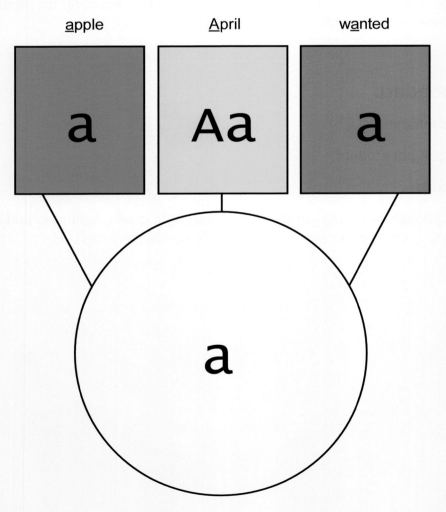

LESSON 2 – LETTER c

The letter in the circle makes two different sounds. In the word <u>came</u> it makes the sound of the letter <u>k</u>. In the word <u>cent</u> it makes the sound of the letter <u>s</u>.

Instruct the student to draw a lowercase <u>k</u> in the first box. The sound of it is the same sound as the letter <u>c</u> in <u>came</u>. Color the box orange. Say the sound of the letter <u>c</u> as in <u>came</u>.

In the second box draw the letter <u>s</u>. The first letter in the word <u>cent</u> makes the sound of the letter <u>s</u>. Color the box orange. Say the sound of the letter <u>c</u> as in <u>cent</u>.

Repeat the two sounds of the letter <u>c</u>

For older students have them write the words above the boxes and underline the letter <u>c</u> in each word.

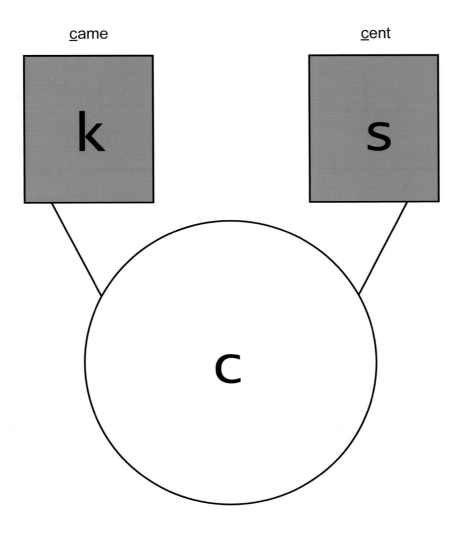

LESSON 3 – LETTERS <u>ch</u>

The letters in the circle make two different sounds: the sound "ch" as in <u>much</u> and the <u>ch</u> in school. Draw the letters <u>ch</u> in the first box. The <u>ch</u> makes the sound "ch" in the word <u>much</u>. Color the box orange. Say the sound "ch" as in the word <u>much</u>.

In the second box draw the letter <u>k</u>. The <u>ch</u> in the word <u>school</u> makes the sound of the letter <u>k</u>. Color the box orange. Say the sound "ch" as in the word <u>school</u>.

Repeat the two sounds of the letters <u>ch</u>.

For older students have them write the words above each box and underline the <u>ch</u> in each word.

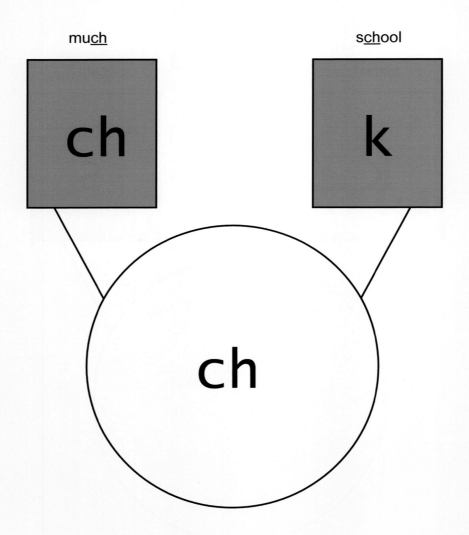

LESSON 4 – LETTER <u>e</u>

The letter in the circle makes two different sounds: "e" as in <u>e</u>nd and "e" as in m<u>e</u>. Instruct the students to draw a lowercase <u>e</u> in the first box. This letter makes the sound "e" as in the first letter of the word <u>e</u>nd. Color the box light green to represent the short vowel sound. Say the sound "e" as in <u>e</u>nd.

In the second box draw an uppercase <u>E</u> and a lowercase <u>e</u>. The letters in this box make the sound "e" as in the word m<u>e</u>. Color the box yellow to represent the long vowel sound. Say the sound "e" as in m<u>e</u>.

Repeat the two sounds of the letter <u>e</u>.

For older students have them write the words above each box and underline the letter <u>e</u> in each word.

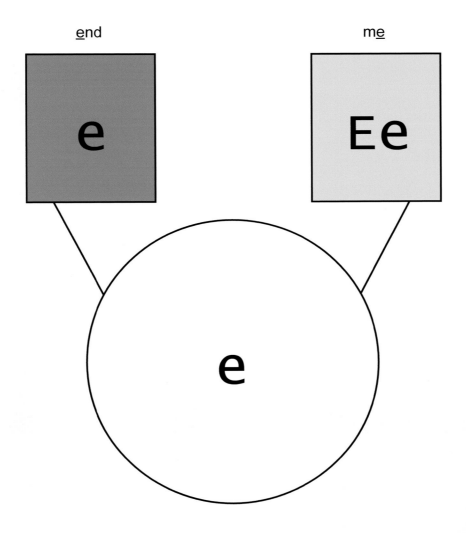

LESSON 5 – LETTERS <u>ea</u>

   The letters in the circle make three different sounds: "ea" as in <u>eat</u>, "ea" as in <u>head</u> and "ea" as in <u>break</u>. Instruct the students to draw an uppercase <u>E</u> and a lowercase <u>e</u> in the first box. These letters make the sound "ea" as in <u>eat</u>. Color the box yellow to represent the long vowel sound. Say the sound "ea" as in <u>eat</u>.

   In the center box draw the letter <u>e</u> in lowercase. This letter makes the sound "ea" as in <u>head</u>. Color the box light green to represent the short vowel sound. Say the sound "ea" as in <u>head</u>.

   In the third box draw a uppercase <u>A</u> and a lowercase <u>a</u>. These letters make the "ea" sound in the word <u>break</u>. Color the box yellow to represent the long vowel sound. Say the sound "ea" as in <u>break</u>.

   Repeat the three sounds of the letters <u>ea</u>.

   For older students have them write the words above each box and underline the letters <u>ea</u> in each word.

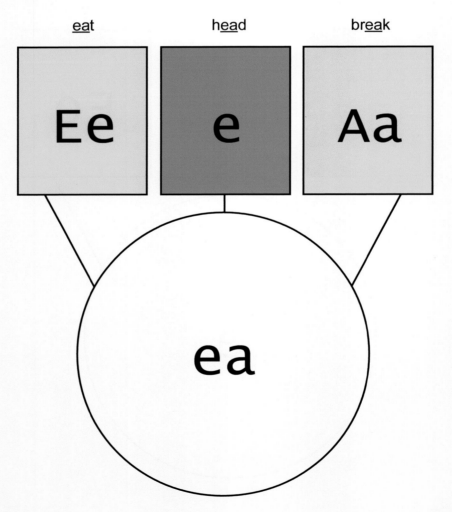

LESSON 6 – LETTERS ed

The letters in the circle make three different sounds: "ed" as in graded, "ed" as in loved and "ed" as in wrecked. Draw the letters ed in lowercase in the first box. These letters make the sound "ed" as in graded. Color the box orange. Say the sound "ed" as in graded.

In the second box draw the lowercase letter d, the ed makes the sound "d" as in loved. Color the box orange. Say the sound "d" as in loved.

In the third box draw the lowercase t, the ed makes the sound "t" as in wrecked. Color the box orange. Say the sound "t" as in wrecked.

Repeat the sounds of the letters ed.

For older students have them write the words above the boxes and underline the letters ed in each word.

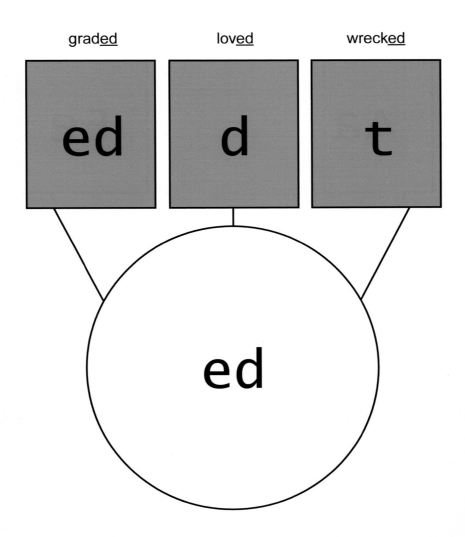

LESSON 7 - LETTERS <u>ei</u>

The letters in the circle make two different sounds: "ei" as in <u>eight</u> and "ei" as in <u>conceit</u>. Draw an uppercase <u>A</u> and <u>a</u> lowercase a in the first box, these letters make the sound "ei" as in <u>eight</u>. Color the box yellow to represent the long vowel sound. Say the sound "ei" as in the word <u>eight</u>.

In the second box draw an uppercase <u>E</u> and a lowercase <u>e</u>. These letters make the sound "ei" as in <u>conceit</u>. Color the box yellow to represent the long vowel sound. Say the sound "ei" as in the word <u>conceit</u>.

Repeat the sound of the letter <u>ei</u>.

For older students have them write the words above each box and underline the <u>ei</u> in each word.

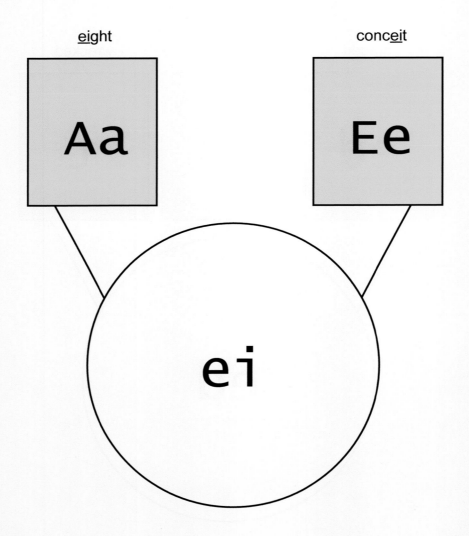

LESSON 8 – LETTERS ew

The letters in the circle have two different sounds: "ew" as in <u>grew</u> and "ew" as in <u>ewe</u>. Draw two lowercase o in the first box. Color the box light blue. Say the sound "ew" as in <u>grew</u>.

In the second box draw an uppercase <u>U</u> and a lowercase <u>u</u>. These letters make the sound "ew" as in the word <u>ewe</u>. Color the box yellow to represent the long vowel sound. Say the sound "ew" as in the word <u>ewe</u>.

Repeat the sounds of the letters <u>ew</u>.

For older students have them write the words above the boxes and underline the letter <u>ew</u> in each word.

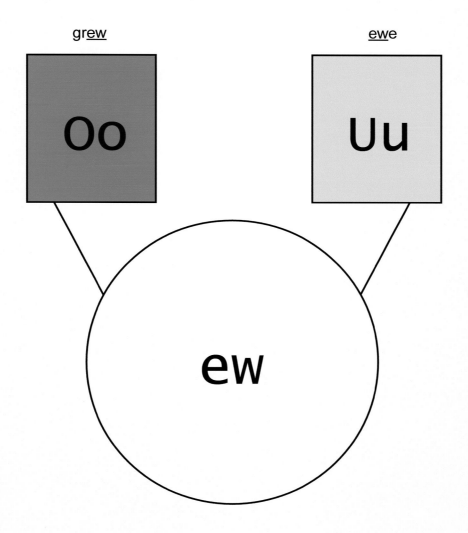

gr<u>ew</u>   <u>ew</u>e

Oo   Uu

ew

LESSON 9 – LETTERS <u>ey</u>

The letters in the circle make two different sounds: "ey" as in <u>key</u> and "ey" as in <u>they</u>. Draw an uppercase <u>E</u> and a lowercase <u>e</u> in the first box. These letters make the "ey" sound as in <u>key</u>. Color the box yellow to represent the long vowel sound. Say the sound "ey" as in <u>key</u>.

In the second box draw an uppercase <u>A</u> and a lowercase <u>a</u>. These letters make the "ey" sound as in <u>they</u>. Color the box yellow to represent the long vowel sound. Say the sound "ey" as in <u>they</u>.

Repeat the two sounds of the letters <u>ey</u>.

For older students have them write the words above each box and underline the <u>ey</u> in each word.

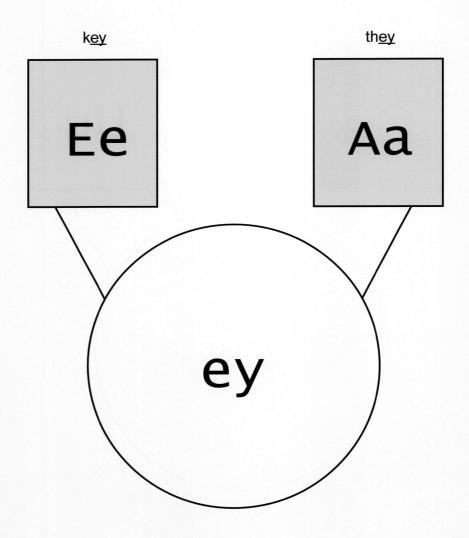

LESSON 10 – LETTER g

The letter in the circle makes two different sounds: "g" as in <u>g</u>irl and "g" as in <u>g</u>em. Draw a lowercase <u>g</u> in the first box. This letter makes the sound "g" as in <u>g</u>irl. Color the box orange. Say the sound "g" as in <u>g</u>irl.

In the second box draw a lowercase <u>j</u>. The letter <u>g</u> in <u>g</u>em makes the sound "j" like the letter <u>j</u>. Color the box orange. Say the sound "g" as in <u>g</u>em.

Repeat the two sounds of the letter <u>g</u>.

For older students have them write the words above the boxes and underline the letter <u>g</u> in each word.

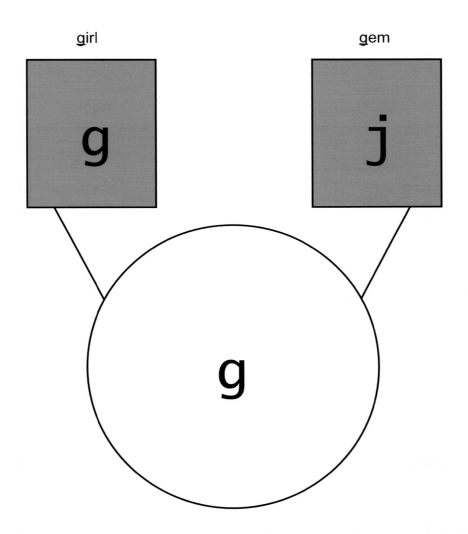

LESSON 11 – LETTERS <u>gh</u>

The letters in the circle make three different sounds. The letters gh make the sound "g" in <u>ghost</u>, the <u>gh</u> in <u>laugh</u> makes the sound of the letter <u>f</u>, and the gh in the word <u>night</u> is silent. Draw a lowercase <u>g</u> in the first box. This letter makes the sound "gh" in <u>ghost</u>. Color the box orange. Say the sound "gh" as in <u>ghost</u>.

In the second box draw the letter <u>f</u>. The <u>f</u> makes the sound of the <u>gh</u> in <u>laugh</u>. Color the box orange. Say the sound "gh" as in <u>laugh</u>.

In the third box write the word <u>silent</u>. The <u>gh</u> in the word <u>night</u> is silent. Color the box orange. Don't make a "gh" sound here because it is silent, just smile!

Repeat the sounds of the <u>gh</u>.

For older students have them write the words above each box and underline the letter gh in each word.

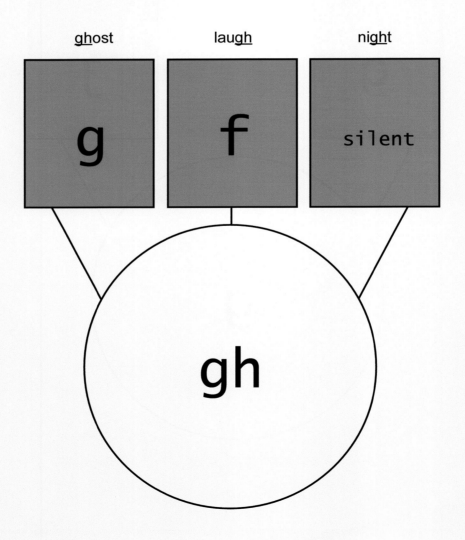

LESSON 12 – LETTER i̲

The letter in the circle makes two different sounds: "i" as in I̲ndian and "i" as in i̲sland. Draw a lowercase i̲ in the first box, this letter makes the sound of the first letter in I̲ndian. Color the box light green to represent the short vowel sound. Say the sound "i" as in I̲ndian.

In the second box draw an uppercase I̲ and a lowercase i̲ . These letters make the sound of the first letter in i̲sland. Color the box yellow to represent the long vowel sound. Say the sound "i" as in i̲sland.

Repeat the two sounds of the letter i̲.

For older students have them write the words above the boxes and underline the first letter i̲ in each word.

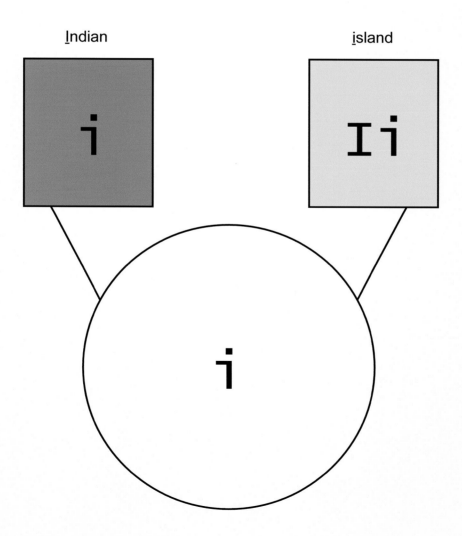

I̲ndian   i̲sland

LESSON 13 – LETTERS <u>ie</u>

The letters in the circle make three different sounds: "ie" as in <u>pie</u>, "ie" as in <u>friend</u> and "ie as in <u>field</u>. Draw an uppercase <u>I</u> and a lowercase <u>i</u> in the first box. These letters make the sound of the <u>ie</u> in <u>pie</u>. Color the box yellow to represent the long vowel sound. Say the sound "ie" as in <u>pie</u>.

In the second box draw a lowercase <u>e</u>, this letter makes the sound of the <u>ie</u> in <u>friend</u>. Color the box light green to represent the short vowel sound. Say the sound "ie" as in <u>friend</u>.

In the third box draw an uppercase <u>E</u> and a lowercase <u>e</u>. These letters make the sound of the <u>ie</u> in the word <u>field</u>. Color the box yellow to represent the long vowel sound. Say the sound "ie" as in <u>field</u>.

Repeat the three sounds of the letters <u>ie</u>.

For older students have them write the words above the boxes and underline the letters <u>ie</u> in each word.

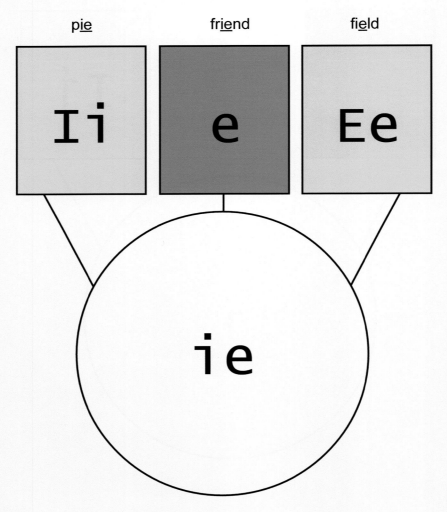

LESSON 14 – LETTER o

The letter in the circle makes three different sounds: "o" as in <u>o</u>dd, "o" as in <u>o</u>pen and "o" as in d<u>o</u>. Draw a lowercase <u>o</u> in the first box. This letter makes the sound "o" as in <u>o</u>dd. Color the box light green to represent the short vowel sound. Say the sound "o" as in odd.

In the second box draw an uppercase O and a lowercase o. This letter makes the sound "o" as in open. Color the box yellow to represent the long vowel sound. Say "o" as in <u>o</u>pen.

In the third box draw two lowercase <u>o</u>. These letters make the sound "o" as in d<u>o</u>. Color the box light blue. Say the "o" as in d<u>o</u>.

Repeat the three sounds of the letter <u>o</u>.

For older students have them write the words above each box and underline the letter <u>o</u> in each word.

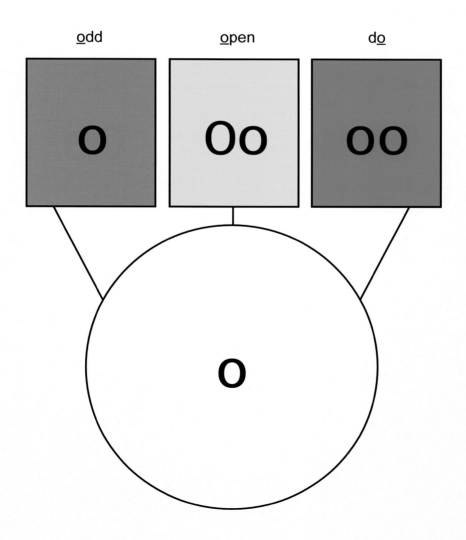

LESSON 15 – LETTERS <u>oo</u>

The letters in the circle make three different sounds: "oo" as in <u>goo</u>, "oo" as in <u>flood</u>, and "oo" as in <u>floor</u>. Draw two lowercase <u>o</u> in the first box. These letters make the sound "oo" as in <u>goo</u>. Color the box light blue. Say the sound "oo" as in <u>goo</u>.

In the second box draw a lowercase <u>u</u>. This letter makes the sound of the <u>oo</u> in the word <u>flood</u>. Color the box light green to represent the short vowel sound. Say the sound "oo" as in <u>flood</u>.

In the third box draw an uppercase <u>O</u> and a lowercase <u>o</u>. These letters make the sound "oo" as in <u>floor</u>. Color the box yellow to represent the long vowel sound. Say the sound "oo" as in <u>floor</u>.

Repeat the three sound of the letters <u>oo</u>.

For older students have them write the words above the boxes and underline the <u>oo</u> in each word.

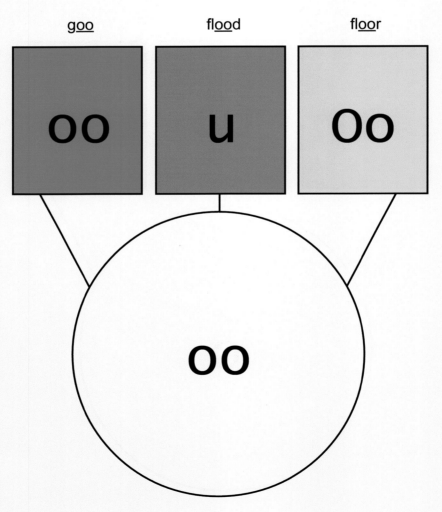

LESSON 16 – LETTERS <u>ou</u>

The letters in the circle make four different sounds: "ou" as in <u>round</u>, "ou" as in <u>four</u>, "ou" as in <u>you</u> and "ou" as in <u>country</u>. Draw lowercase <u>ow</u> in the first box. This makes the sound "ou" as in <u>round</u>. Color the box light blue. Say the sound "ou" as in <u>round</u>.

In the top box to the right draw an uppercase <u>O</u> and a lowercase <u>o</u>. This makes the sound "ou" as in <u>four</u>. Color the box yellow to represent the long vowel sound. Say the sound "ou" as in <u>four</u>.

In the left bottom box draw two <u>o</u>. These make the sound of the "ou" in the word <u>you</u>. Color the box light blue. Say the sound ""ou" as in <u>you</u>.

In the bottom right box draw a lowercase <u>u</u>. This letter makes the sound "ou" as in <u>country</u>. Color the letter light green to represent the short vowel sound. Say the sound "ou" as in <u>country</u>.

Repeat all four sounds of the letters ou.

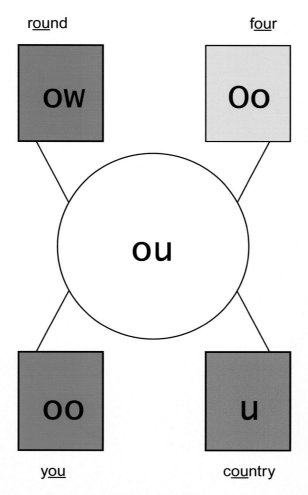

Older students - write and underline the words above and below the boxes.

LESSON 17 – LETTERS <u>ow</u>

The letters in the circle make two different sounds: "ow" as in <u>how</u> and "ow" as in <u>low</u>. Draw the lowercase letters <u>ow</u> in the first box. They make the sound "ow" as in <u>how</u>. Color the box light blue. Say the sound "ow" as in <u>how</u>.

In the second box draw an uppercase <u>O</u> and a lowercase <u>o</u>. These make the sound of "ow" as in <u>low</u>. Color the box yellow to represent the long vowel sound. Say the sound "ow" as in <u>low</u>.

Repeat the two sounds of the letters <u>ow</u>.

For older students have them write the words above the boxes and underline the letters <u>ow</u> in each word.

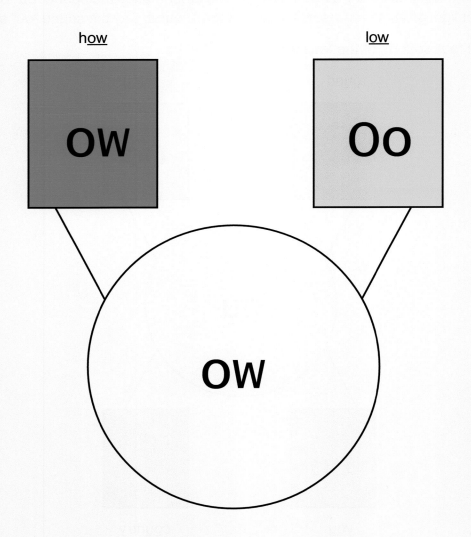

LESSON 18 – LETTER <u>s</u>

The letter in the circle makes two different sounds: <u>s</u> as in <u>us</u> and the sound of the letter <u>z</u> in the word <u>as</u>. Draw a lowercase <u>s</u> in the first box. The letter makes the sound "s" in the word <u>us</u>. Color the box orange. Say the sound "s" as in <u>us</u>.

In the second box draw the letter <u>z</u>. The letter <u>s</u> in the word <u>as</u> makes the sound of the letter <u>z.</u> Color the box orange. Say the sound "s" as in the word <u>as</u>.

Repeat the two sounds of the letter <u>s</u>.

For older students have them write the words above the boxes and underline the letter <u>s</u> in each word.

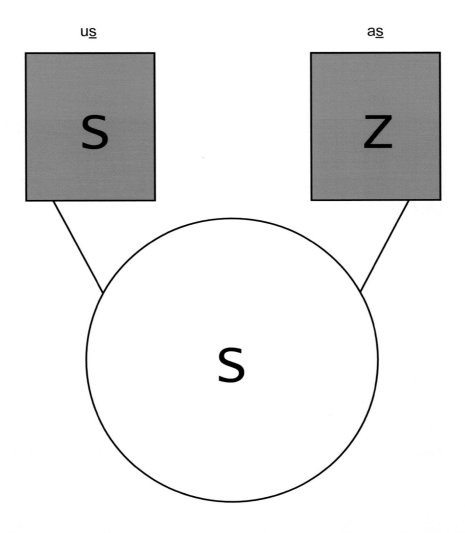

LESSON 19 – LETTER <u>u</u>

The letter in the circle makes three sounds: "u" as in <u>up</u>, "u" as in <u>music</u> and "u" as in <u>put</u>. Draw a lowercase <u>u</u> in the first box. This letter makes the sound of the <u>u</u> in <u>up</u>. Color the box light green to represent the short vowel sound. Say the "u" as in <u>us</u>.

In the second box draw an uppercase <u>U</u> and a lowercase <u>u.</u> These letters make the sound of the letter <u>u</u> in the word <u>music</u>. Color the box yellow to represent the long vowel sound. Say the sound "u" as in <u>music</u>.

In the third box draw two <u>o</u>. These letters make the sound "u" as in put. Color the box light blue. Say the sound "u" as in <u>put</u>.

Repeat the three sounds of the letter <u>u</u>.

For older students have them write the words above the boxes and underline the letter <u>u</u> in each word.

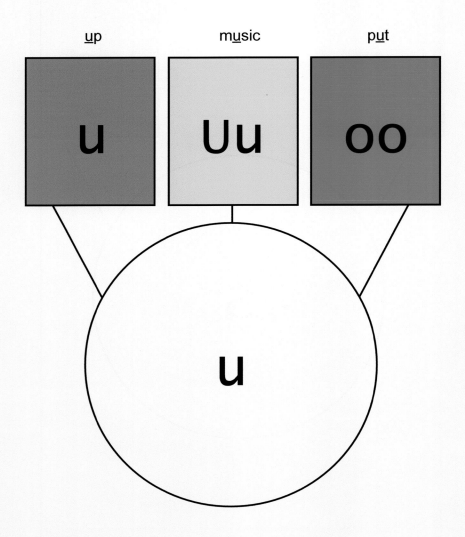

LESSON 20 – LETTERS <u>ui</u>

The letters in the circle make two different sounds: "ui" as in <u>fruit</u> and "ui" as in <u>suit</u>. Draw two <u>o</u> in the first box. These make the sound of the <u>ui</u> in <u>fruit</u>. Color the box light blue. Say the sound "ui" as in <u>fruit</u>.

In the second box draw an uppercase <u>U</u> and a lowercase <u>u</u>. These make the sound of "ui" in <u>suit</u>. Color the box yellow to represent the long vowel sound. Say the sound "ui" as in <u>suit</u>.

Repeat the two sounds of the letters <u>ui</u>.

For older students have them write the words above the boxes and underline the <u>ui</u> in each word.

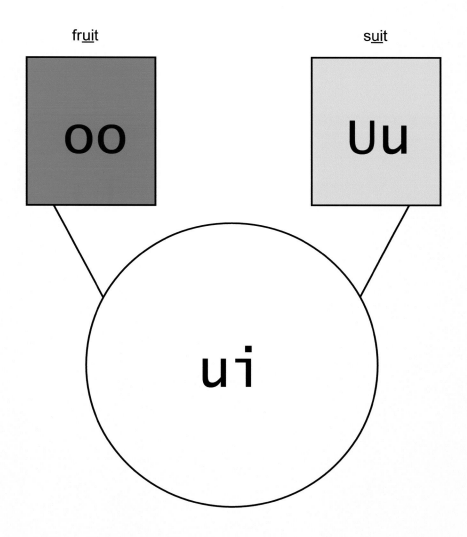

LESSON 21 – LETTER y

The letter in the circle makes three different sounds: "y" as in yellow, "y" as in baby and "y" as in my. Draw a lowercase y in the first box. This letter makes the sound "y" in the word yellow. Color the box orange. Say the sound "y" as in yellow.

In the second box draw an uppercase E and a lowercase e. These letters make the sound "y" in the word baby. Color the box yellow to represent the long vowel sound. Say the sound "y' as in baby.

In the third box draw an uppercase I and a lowercase i. These letters make the sound "y" in the word my. Color the box yellow to represent the long vowel sound. Say the sound "y" as in my.

Repeat the three sounds of the letter y.

For the older students have them write the words above the boxes and underline the y in each word,

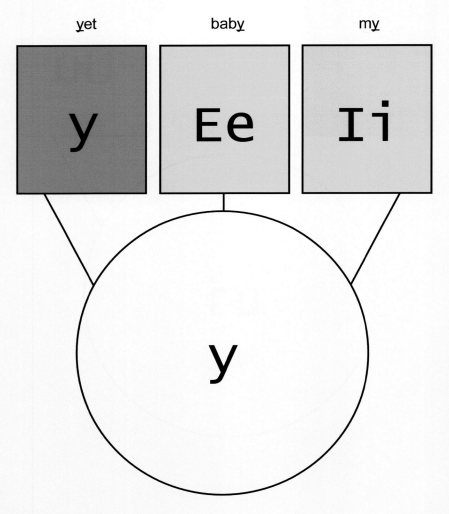

LESSON 22 – MORE LETTERS WITH SAME SPELLINGS BUT DIFFERENT SOUNDS

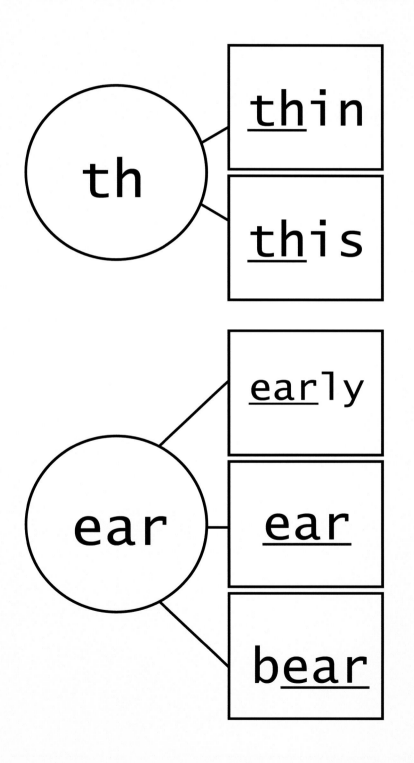

LESSON 23 – LETTERS <u>ough</u>

"o" th<u>ough</u>

"oo" thr<u>ough</u>

"uf" r<u>ough</u>

"off" c<u>ough</u>

"aw" th<u>ough</u>t

"ow" b<u>ough</u>

Appendix

DIFFERENT SPELLINGS FOR THE LONG A SOUND

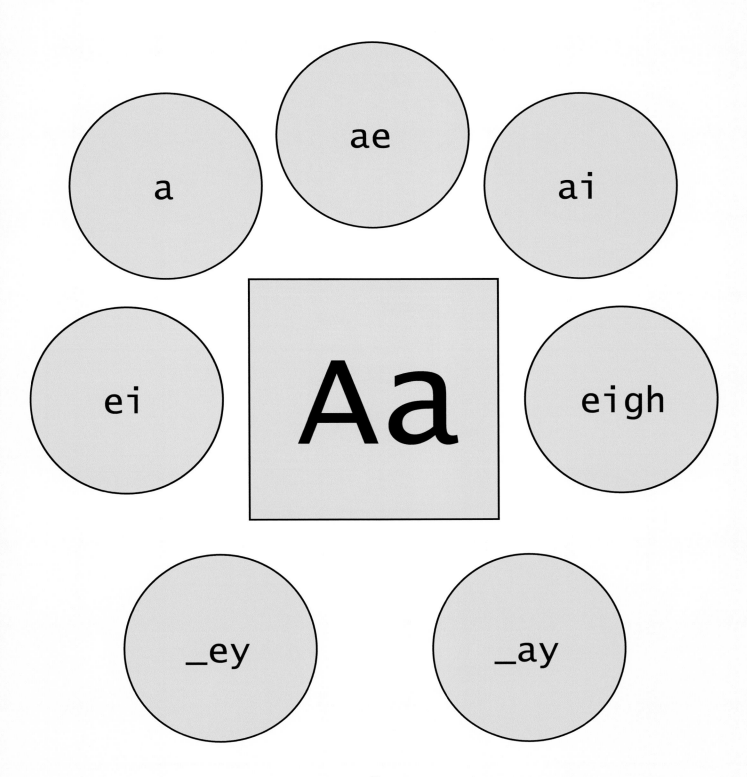

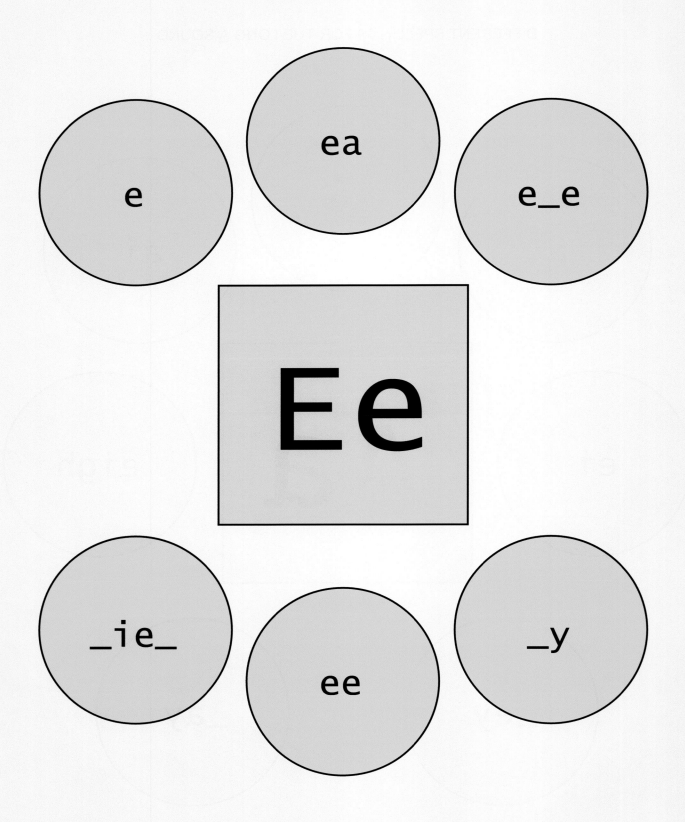

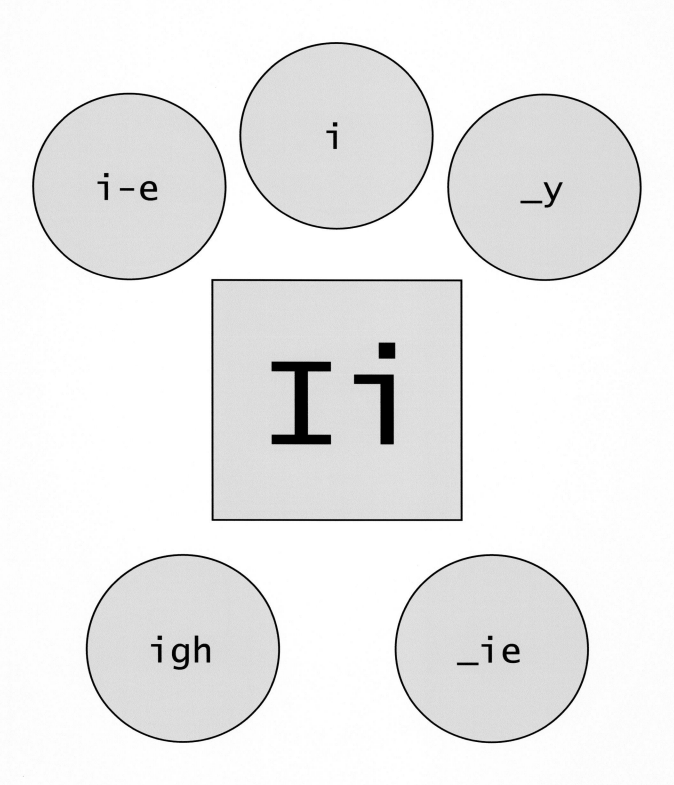

DIFFERENT SPELLINGS FOR THE LONG O SOUND

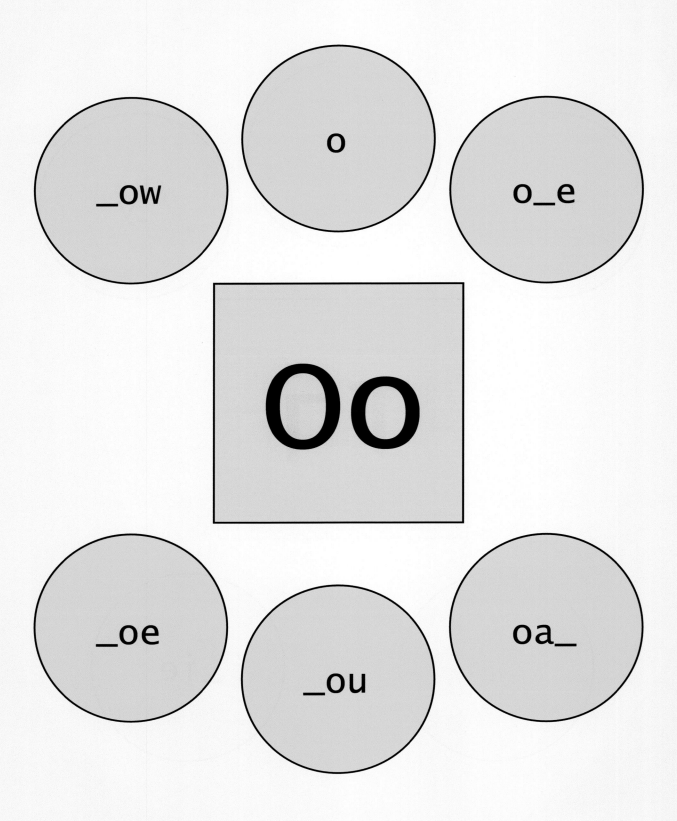

DIFFERENT SPELLINGS FOR THE LONG U SOUND

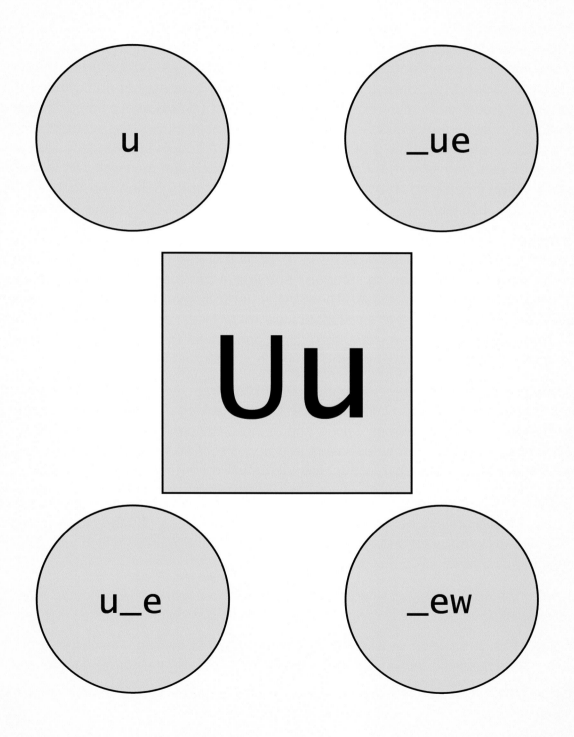

Author's Note

I am a "special" person. I was diagnosed with Bipolar Disorder in my late 30s. Because of this diagnosis I thought my life was over and that I would never be able to succeed in life nor accomplish my dreams for the future. Here I was now 40 years old, married and with two young sons to raise. I had always believed that I should be a stay-at-home mom. So I did not seek employment once my children were born. Then I heard about homeschooling and looked into it. I acquired educational materials and was able to use these materials to teach my eldest son to read well at the age of 4. I taught him Preschool and Kindergarten at home using the book *Learning at Home: Preschool & Kindergarten* and the book *The Writing Road to Reading*. When he entered first grade at La Gloria Elementary School, his teacher, Ms. Lori Jones would send him into the second grade GATE program classroom for his reading lessons.

At the age of 45 I decided to put my sons in a private school where I began working as an instructional aide in my eldest son's classroom. It was there that my dream returned to me to become a teacher. So the following summer I enrolled at Hartnell College taking a couple of ECE classes and a psychology class. There in the psychology class I met my professor who introduced me to the department for students with disabilities, and I felt that I would benefit from it. This professor became my counselor and confidant for the next three years that it took me to earn my A.A. degree. I also earned the honor of Magna Cum Laude.

Following graduation I received scholarships and help from the California State Department of Rehabilitation and I entered California State University Monterey Bay. Because of issues with the Bipolar Disorder I was only taking one to three classes per semester. Finally, at the age of 55, while I was taking my last class in order to receive my B.A. in Liberal Studies, I became ill again and had to leave school with an unfulfilled dream.

At the age of 60 I have returned to the university to take that last class. The book you have in your hands is the project that I have accomplished in the class. By the time you read this, I will have already graduated and received my B.A. in Liberal Studies which will allow me to be a substitute teacher.

I give God, first of all, my gratitude and praise because without Him I could never have accomplished all this. "I can do all things through Christ who strengthens me" (Philippians 4:13).

Spalding, R. B. & Spalding W. T. (1990), The writing road to reading: The Spalding method of phonics for teaching speech, writing and reading. New York, NY: William Morrow and Company, Inc.

Ward, A. (1990), Learning at home: preschool and kindergarten. Gresham, OR: Christian Life Workshops.

Printed in the United States
By Bookmasters